MANUAL ON CLIMATE CHANGE ADJUSTMENTS FOR DETAILED ENGINEERING DESIGN OF ROADS USING EXAMPLES FROM VIET NAM

JUNE 2020

ASIAN DEVELOPMENT BANK

Contents

Tables

Acknowledgments

This step-by-step manual was planned and developed by the Climate Change and Disaster Risk Management Division, Sustainable Development and Climate Change Department (SDCC), of the Asian Development Bank (ADB), in close collaboration with ADB's Southeast Asia Department (SERD).

It was prepared by Robert Wilby, SDCC consultant, who also drafted the accompanying technical document. Both documents benefited from substantive input received from David Salter, principal natural resources and agriculture specialist, SERD; Charles Rodgers, SDCC consultant; and Xianfu Lu, former senior climate change specialist (climate change adaptation), SDCC. Support in their finalization was provided by Arghya Sinha Roy, senior climate change specialist (climate change adaptation), SDCC; Sugar Gonzales, climate change officer (climate change adaptation), SDCC; Mary Ann Asico, editorial consultant; and Edith Creus, layout artist.

Independent technical review by the following SDCC consultants is gratefully recognized: Clive Carpenter, Peter Droogers, Anthony Kiem, and Steven Wade.

This step-by-step manual, as well as the technical document, would also not have been developed without the encouragement and overall guidance of Preety Bhandari, chief of the Climate Change and Disaster Risk Management Thematic Group and concurrently director, Climate Change and Disaster Risk Management Division, SDCC.

Abbreviations

ADB	Asian Development Bank
CMIP5	Coupled Model Intercomparison Project, Phase 5
DED	detailed engineering design
GCM	general circulation model (or global climate model)
IDF	intensity–duration–frequency
IPCC	Intergovernmental Panel on Climate Change
KNMI	Royal Netherlands Meteorological Institute
mm	millimeter
MONRE	Ministry of Natural Resources and Environment, Viet Nam
RCP	representative (greenhouse gas) concentration pathway
Rx1day	1-day annual maximum rainfall total
SLR	sea-level rise
TCVN	national standards issued by the Vietnam Standards and Quality Institute, Ministry of Science and Technology ("TCVN" stands for "Technical Committee of Vietnam")

Executive Summary

Climate change is expected to intensify extreme rainfall and raise global sea levels. Without adaptation and resilience measures, heavier rainfall and higher sea levels are likely to increase river and coastal flooding and erosion risk.

This manual contains step-by-step procedures for incorporating adjustments for climate change at the detailed engineering design (DED) stage of a project. For the full technical rationale and basis of the procedures, see the accompanying knowledge product (ADB 2020a).

Climate change adjustment procedures are demonstrated here through the use of the following:

(i)   1-day annual maximum rainfall total (Rx1day), for hydraulic structures;
(ii) local mean sea-level change and high-water levels, for site evaluation of coastal flooding and erosion risks.

Accompanying Microsoft Excel spreadsheets show how the procedures are implemented in each case, using exemplar road projects in Viet Nam. These principles and practices are intended to be transferable to other sectors, regions, and stages of the asset life cycle (from project concept to decommissioning).

Although climate hazards are treated separately here, it is important to recognize that they can be concurrent. Within the Asia and Pacific region, tropical cyclones bring heavy rainfall, with high wind speeds, waves, and storm surges. Hence, the DED should reflect the possibility of climate-driven changes in *multi*-hazards at a site.

The overall approach is intended to be as transparent as possible. All sources of information and assumptions should be open to scrutiny, given the large uncertainty and rapidly advancing science behind some elements. Input values should be periodically reviewed and refreshed, at least in line with the latest reports of the Intergovernmental Panel on Climate Change (IPCC) and national scenarios.

Some data may be impossible to obtain for project site(s), in which case referral to nearest-neighbor records or published values may be necessary. Again, transparent procedures will reveal such knowledge gaps and highlight opportunities for further research.

Unfortunately, no single source or platform exists for obtaining all the climate change information needed for DED at specific sites. In its absence, there is no alternative to gathering input values from different sources.

Finally, there is a limit to what can be achieved through generic guidance when allowing for site-specific climate threats in DED. Nonetheless, the underlying principles and procedures set out in this manual offer points of departure for more sophisticated assessments of high-risk projects.

1 Introduction

Climate change is expected to intensify heavy rainfall and raise global sea levels. More intense rainfall occurs because a warmer atmosphere holds more water—at least ~6.5% more per degree Celsius, according to the laws of thermodynamics (Allen and Ingram 2002). Higher sea levels result from thermal expansion of the ocean, combined with ice melt from land, local gravity effects, vertical land movements, and changes in ocean currents. Without adaptation and resilience measures, heavier rainfall and higher sea levels are likely to increase river and coastal flooding risk.

All Asian Development Bank (ADB) infrastructure projects now undergo mandatory screening to identify those at high or medium risk of being adversely affected by climate change. At-risk projects must then be "climate-proofed" and made resilient to identified climate change impact. Some adaptations may involve adjustments to engineered structures, including urban drainage systems, flood levees, and coastal defenses.

National engineering design standards are routinely based on intensity–duration–frequency (IDF) tables for hydrologic events. These tables provide extreme-value estimates for variables such as heavy rainfall, sea level, storm-surge height, wind speed, wave height, and air and water temperature. Such values were previously estimated from statistical distributions fitted to historical records, with a stationary time series as the key assumption. Now, adjustments to extreme-value distributions must be based on expected changes in the same quantities shown by climate models.

This manual contains step-by-step procedures for adjusting the detailed engineering design (DED) of a project to take climate change into account. For the full technical rationale and basis of the procedures, see the accompanying knowledge product (ADB 2020a). Both documents were drafted within the framework of the guidelines for the Basic Infrastructure for Inclusive Growth projects of the Viet Nam road transport sector and the specific institutional context of those projects. As part of this work, the ADB project preparatory technical assistance (PPTA) team developed climate change–adjusted rainfall projections for use within hydrologic formulas for estimating future peak river flows and flood levels (ADB 2018).

Exact climate variables (of a given duration and return period) are normally mandated by national design standards for structures. In Viet Nam, national standards for roads (TCVN 4054:2005) and bridges (TCVN 9845:2013) require a design flood level of 1 in 100 years for expressways, and 1 in 25 years for category 3, 4, or 5 rural roads. The 1-day annual maximum rainfall total (Rx1day) is a critical variable in all formulas for hydrologic calculations of design water discharge, flood level, and flow velocity.

Sea-level rise (SLR) is an existential threat to populations, coastal infrastructure, and land use worldwide. However, according to World Bank sensitivity analyses, Viet Nam is the country that is the most vulnerable to a 1 meter SLR in terms of exposed population, potential loss in gross domestic product (GDP), and threat to urban areas and wetlands (Dasgupta et al. 2009a). Moreover, a 10% increase in storm-surge height combined with a 1 meter SLR could expand the area of the storm-surge zone in Viet Nam by 35% (Dasgupta et al. 2009b).

This manual demonstrates climate change adjustment procedures using (i) Rx1day for hydraulic structures; and (ii) local mean sea-level change and high-water levels for site evaluations of coastal flooding and erosion risks. Accompanying Microsoft Excel spreadsheets show how the procedures are implemented in each case, using exemplar data for Viet Nam.

The procedures described in this manual are suitable for design events with return periods of up to 25 years; for rarer extreme events, more sophisticated, site-specific analyses are required. A precautionary approach is taken to the use of climate change models, given their uncertainty and recognized limitations (Flato et al. 2013). Here the 97.5th percentile of the climate-model ensemble range is taken for Rx1day, whereas upper-bound estimates are used for extreme sea-level changes. Representative concentration pathway (RCP) 8.5 is used throughout for "permanent projects and long term plans," as recommended by the Viet Nam Ministry of Natural Resources and Environment (MONRE 2016, 89). Furthermore, RCP8.5 reflects business-as-usual emissions (although the choice of emission pathway does not matter until the second half of the 21st century). Unless stated otherwise, all climate-model information originates from the Coupled Model Intercomparison Project, Phase 5 (CMIP5) (Taylor, Stouffer, and Meehl 2012).

2 Extreme-Rainfall Estimation for Hydraulic Structures

This section discusses in broad terms the assumptions and procedures behind extreme-rainfall estimates. The accompanying knowledge product (ADB 2020a) offers a more detailed commentary on the subject, as well as a Further Reading list on the adjustment of extreme sub-daily rainfall estimates and worked examples (Appendixes 1 and 2).

Considerable uncertainty surrounds climate-model projections of extreme rainfall, especially for low-probability, high-impact events. This is because climate models only partially represent extreme weather events (e.g., tropical cyclones) and regional effects of modes of climate variability (e.g., El Niño) (Yun, Yeh, and Ha 2016; Chen et al. 2017). Statistical and dynamic downscaling techniques improve the *precision* of local rainfall scenarios without necessarily increasing their *accuracy*, as the projected changes in heavy rainfall ultimately depend on the realism of the climate models used to drive the downscaling (Pielke and Wilby 2012).

Rainfall uncertainty (up to the mid-21st century) is mainly due to the choice of climate model, combined with natural variability (Hawkins and Sutton 2010; Deser et al. 2014). Where national scenarios have been created, these should be the first point of reference for engineers (e.g., Katzfey, McGregor, and Suppiah 2014; ABOM and CSIRO 2014). However, it is important to keep in mind that high-resolution national scenarios may not reflect the full range of climate uncertainty, given the prohibitive cost of running all combinations of initial conditions, emission scenarios, climate models, and downscaling techniques.

A realistic simulation of the present-day climate is a necessary but insufficient test of the accuracy of future changes in precipitation shown in general circulation models (GCMs) (Knutti et al. 2010) and downscaling (Racherla, Shindell, and Faluvegi 2012). Across Southeast Asia, there are "significant biases" or "implausible" northeast and summer monsoons in the following GCMs: FGOALS-g2;[1] INMCM4;[2] IPSL-CM5B-LR;[3] MIROC-ESM;[4] MIROC-ESM-CHEM;[5] MRI-CGCM3;[6] and Nor-ESM1-M[7] (McSweeney et al. 2015). Other models with errors in atmospheric circulation over the region are MIROC5, ACCESS1-3, and IPSL-CM5A-LR. These climate models are excluded from the rainfall analysis in this manual.

---

[1] Flexible Global Ocean–Atmosphere–Land System Model, Grid-point Version 2.
[2] Russian Institute for Numerical Mathematics Climate Model Version 4.
[3] Low-resolution Institut Pierre Simon Laplace Earth System Model.
[4] Japan Agency for Marine-Earth Science and Technology Earth System Model.
[5] An atmospheric chemistry–coupled version of MIROC-ESM.
[6] A climate model developed by the Meteorological Research Institute in Japan.
[7] Norwegian Earth System Model.

Given the uncertainty in rainfall modeling and downscaling, project teams should apply TWO important principles: (i) *transparency* in the choice of climate model(s), downscaling technique(s), and emission scenarios applied; and (ii) *clarity* of any implicit or explicit assumptions made when calculating a design variable. Furthermore, all tables of climate change adjustments should be subject to periodic review to benefit from advances in climate science. With these principles in place, adjustments for Rx1day can be obtained from CMIP5 output, as shown in the following sections. The worked example is presented in a series of steps (with accompanying text boxes), and the workflow as a whole is summarized in Table 1.

STEP R1: Specify project objectives.

The project objectives should be clearly stated and should specify the level of climate risk and variables involved, the life of the project, the amount of lock-in (irreversibility), and the degree of precaution required (ADB 2020b). In other words, it is important to begin by understanding the most significant risks to the project objectives, output, and outcomes, rather than with climate-model projections (which come later).

> The exemplar project involves the design of concrete culverts draining river crossings along the Bao Ninh–Hai Ninh coastal road in Quang Binh Province, North Central Coast Region. The expected service life of the culverts is 10 years and the standard of protection for a rural road in Viet Nam is for a 25-year flood (TCVN 4054:2005). The key design variable used for flood estimation is Rx1day.

STEP R2: Check for contextual climate risks at the project concept stage.

Climate-risk screening should consider potential far-field as well as near-field threats to the proposed structure. These include both the direct and the indirect impact of climate change.

Some stretches of the proposed coastal road are only 4 meters (m) above mean sea level or within 100 m of the shoreline. In this case, by focusing on climate adjustments to design criteria for *individual* culverts, project planners may overlook *wider* risks of inundation and erosion of low-lying sections of the road. Other, less exposed routes and access points should be considered at the project concept stage. For the purpose of this exercise, it is assumed that no viable alternatives exist.

A low-lying section of the Bao Ninh–Hai Ninh coastal road.
Map data: Google, DigitalGlobe.

STEP R3: Obtain design values from historical data.

Observed daily rainfall series for the site, especially spurious values that could affect extreme-value estimates, should undergo quality assurance tests (see Further Reading section of this manual). Where there are no data for the site, records for the nearest neighbor may be used. Gridded and interpolated rainfall data will tend to underestimate extreme values and should be avoided except for large river basins. Annual maximum series are then extracted and fitted to an extreme-value distribution such as the Gumbel or other generalized extreme-value distributions. IDF tables may already be available for the site or region. Even so, published values should be subjected to sanity checks against known extreme events.

> According to ADB (2018, 51) the observed Rx1day with 25-year return period is 338 millimeters (mm) for Quang Binh Province. By comparison, a maximum daily rainfall of 502 mm was recorded in the neighboring province of Ha Tinh during the landfall of typhoon Kit (27 September 1978), and a maximum daily rainfall of 394 mm during the landfall of typhoon Lex (27 October 1983).

STEP R4: Download climate change scenarios for the design variable(s).

In 2016, the Ministry of Natural Resources and Environment (MONRE 2016) issued climate change scenarios for Viet Nam based on nine CMIP5 climate models and five dynamic downscaling methods. ADB (2018) applied rainfall scenarios drawn from a subset of three climate models (CNRM-CM5,[8] GFDL-CM3,[9] and HadGEM2-ES[10]) and one downscaling model (the PRECIS Regional Climate Modeling System). Here the full CMIP5 ensemble is downloaded, then a subset of credible climate models is selected on the basis of an evaluation by McSweeney et al. (2015). The resulting 16 climate models characterize modeling uncertainty (but without downscaling). Annual Rx1day series are extracted for each of these climate models, for the whole of Viet Nam, covering the period 1850–2100 under RCP8.5.

> Rx1day series (1850–2100) for Viet Nam were downloaded from the CMIP5 extremes ensemble under RCP8.5, using the setup shown below for KNMI Climate Explorer (http://climexp.knmi.nl/plot_atlas_form.py). The climate-model output is delivered as a zip file with separate subfolders for 1850–2005 and 2006–2100. Individual model results are provided in each subfolder for the specified RCP8.5 scenario. (Note that some climate-model runs begin in 1860 or 1861.) Data are available for 24 CMIP5 climate models, from which a subset of 16 credible climate models was used in the following analysis. Other potential sources of climate-model information are listed in an ADB compendium.
>
> *continued on next page*

---

[8]   Earth system model developed jointly by the French National Meteorological Service and the European Centre for Research and Advanced Training in Scientific Computation.

[9]   Coupled climate model developed at the Geophysical Fluid Dynamics Laboratory of the US National Oceanic and Atmospheric Administration.

[10]   UK Meteorological Office Hadley Centre Earth System Model.

continued from previous page

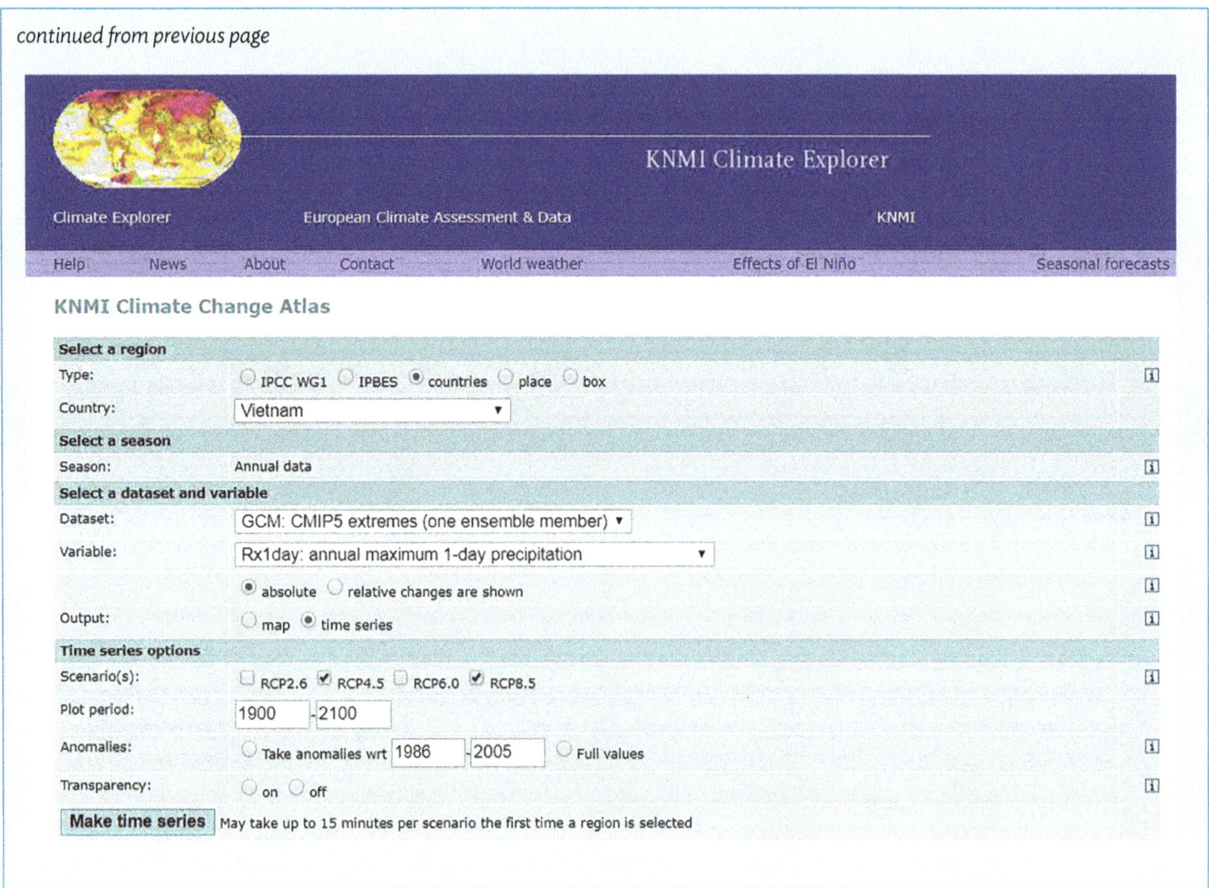

STEP R5: Calculate design values for the specified baseline and future periods.

A standard baseline (1986–2005) is used in evaluating projected changes in Rx1day by 2016–2035 (a 20-year period extending over the expected useful life of the road). (Note that at least 20 years is needed for both baseline and future periods to obtain robust estimates of the required values.) As in Step R3, an extreme-value distribution is fitted separately to the Rx1day series of each climate model and period (in this case, 2 periods x 16 models = 32 distributions). The Rx1day value is then estimated at the specified return period for each climate model and period, along with the 95% confidence range of the extreme-value estimate.

For illustrative purposes, a Gumbel distribution was fitted to each Rx1day series obtained from 16 climate models and two periods (1986–2005 and 2016–2035) in the CMIP5 ensemble to estimate the 25-year return period Rx1day.

There are large variations in Rx1day among the various models due to natural climate variability, as well as differences in grid resolution and physical process representation. Among these models, seven show reductions and nine have increases in the 25-year return period Rx1day (see below). Most changes by the 2030s are still within the range of model uncertainty. (Note also that even the largest Rx1day values are smaller than observed [338 mm] because gridded climate-model output is being compared with a point rainfall measurement.)

There is also uncertainty in the extreme value due to the type of distribution and estimation of distribution parameters (see ADB 2020a, Appendix 1). Here the Gumbel 95% confidence interval is used to show an upper-bound estimate of Rx1day for each climate model (denoted by the T-bars below). The upper-bound Rx1day value can be used to incorporate additional contingency in the design.

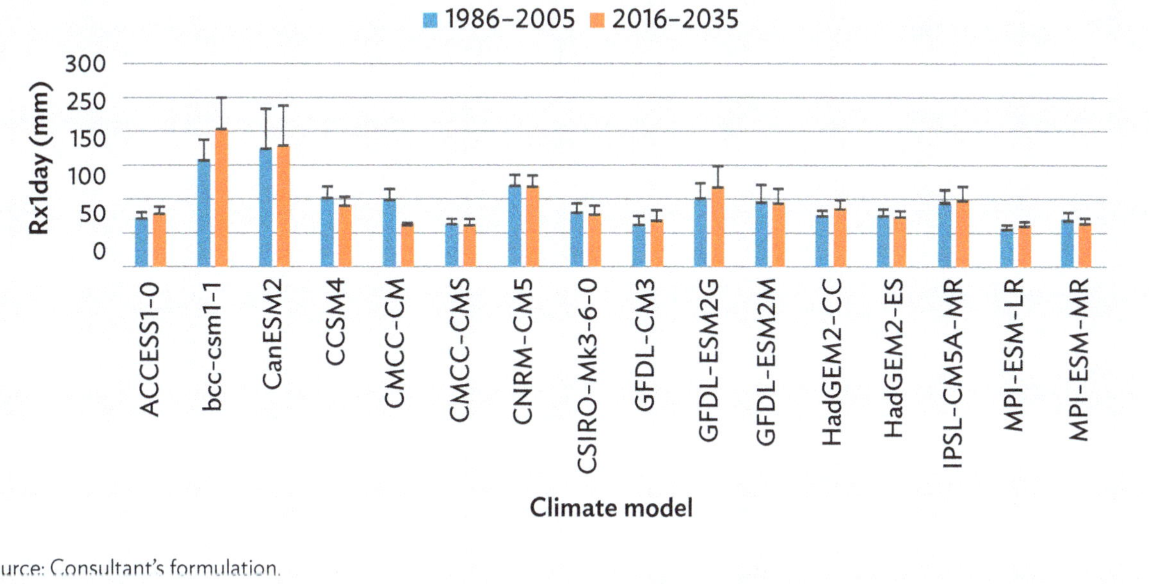

Source: Consultant's formulation.

STEP R6: Derive the change factor for the design variable.

Coarse-resolution climate models are not expected to replicate the observed Rx1day (as noted above). However, it is generally assumed that the *change* signal in climate-model output between the baseline and future periods is robust (and that model biases cancel each other out). The ensemble provides a distribution of expected changes in Rx1day that can then be used to define a change factor at the specified confidence level.

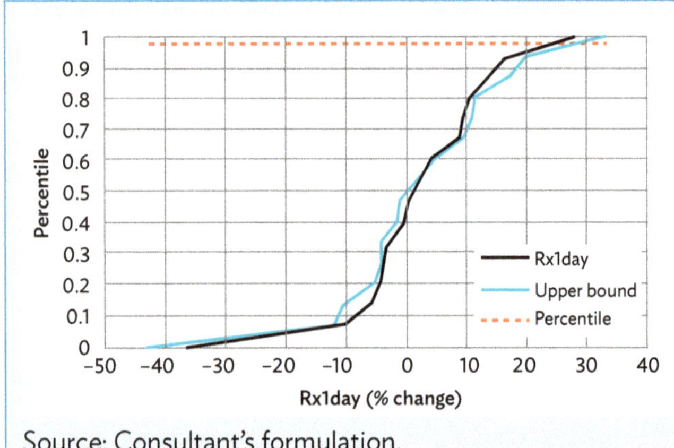

Rx1day varies by −37% to +28% in the CMIP5 subset when the baseline estimates are compared with those for 2016–2035. The 97.5th percentile of the ensemble is +24%. When rounded up to the nearest 5% to avoid undue precision, the recommended change factor for Rx1day is +25%. The upper-bound estimate is +30%.

Source: Consultant's formulation.

STEP R7: Calculate the new design value.

The change factor from Step R6 is used to rescale the observed baseline value. It is assumed that the change signal at the climate-model resolution is the same as the change signal at the local scale. No bias correction or downscaling is used to reduce discrepancies between the climate model and the observed design value.

From Step R3, the observed Rx1day with 25-year return period is 338 mm. From Step R6, the rounded climate change adjustment factor from CMIP5 is +25%. Hence, the climate-adjusted value for Rx1day becomes: 338 x 1.25 = 423 mm. This design value is used with regional flood estimation techniques and standard hydraulic equations to calculate the required culvert dimensions, given the expected discharge, flow depths, and flow velocities at each site (see ADB 2020a, Appendix 2). The upper-bound change factor (+30%) includes an additional margin for the uncertainty in the extreme-value estimate, in this case yielding 338 x 1.3 = 439 mm.

The overall approach is risk-averse. This is justified on the grounds that (i) the procedures may be applied to structures with longer design life; (ii) there is large uncertainty in the magnitude, and sometimes even the sign, of projected regional precipitation changes; and (iii) there is strong observational evidence (Guerreiro et al. 2018) and a physical basis for expecting large increases in precipitation *extremes* linked to rising atmospheric moisture content (Allen and Ingram 2002). For these reasons, climate model ensemble-mean changes in precipitation should not be used.

Steps R1 to R7 involve several simplifying assumptions. These should be disclosed in the resulting documentation of the DED. The caveats are as follows: (i) *changes* in extreme-rainfall projections are accurately represented by the selected climate models; (ii) the model ensemble and the emission scenario adequately characterize the range of epistemic (limited knowledge) and aleatory (unknowable chance) uncertainty; (iii) uncertainties due to observational data and choice of extreme-value distribution can be ignored; (iv) uncertainties from the models/equations used in calculating design variables (e.g., flood discharge, flow velocity) can be neglected; and (v) natural climate variability is represented by the different initial conditions within the climate-model ensemble.

Table 1: Steps in Estimating Design Values for Future Extreme Rainfall

Step	Activity	Viet Nam Example
R1	Specify project **objectives**	Upgrade culverts beneath a coastal road with expected operating life of 10 years. Under Viet Nam Standards TCVN 4054:2005 (for road geometry), a culvert for a category 3, 4, or 5 rural road must be designed to convey discharge generated by an annual maximum 1-day rainfall event (Rx1day) with a 25-year return period.
R2	Check for **contextual climate risks** at the project concept stage and adjust the site selection or design accordingly	Recognize that the most significant threat to the coastal road may not be from fluvial flooding but from storm surge and extreme waves—see the worked example for mean and extreme sea-level change (Table 2).
R3	Obtain the **design value(s)** from historical rainfall data by (a) collating and ensuring the quality of observed data for the site; (b) extracting the annual maximum series; (c) fitting an extreme-value distribution to (b); and (d) calculating the rainfall amount for the required return period with standard error of the estimate.	For the nearest available station: (a) Obtain daily rainfall series and ensure data quality through standard checks (of such items as unexpected outliers, or 5/10 or day-of-week biases); (b) Extract the Rx1day value for each calendar year; (c) Fit an extreme-value distribution (such as Gumbel or GEV) to the annual series in (b); and (d) Use the extreme-value distribution parameters from (c) to estimate the 25-year return period Rx1day with confidence intervals. Here the estimated 25-year Rx1day value is 338 mm.
R4	Download **climate change scenarios** for the design variable(s)	Refer to the latest national climate change scenarios (if available) or the most recent IPCC scenarios. Specify the level of uncertainty in climate projections that must be accommodated (level of risk aversion). This determines the emission scenario and the part(s) of the ensemble range to be evaluated—here the upper-bound 97.5 percentile of an RCP8.5 CMIP5 ensemble. Download the full (1850–2100) Rx1day series from the RCP8.5 CMIP5 ensemble using a tool such as KNMI Climate Explorer. Select the most credible climate models on the basis of ability to simulate present climate processes.
R5	Calculate the **design values** for specified baseline and future periods by repeating Steps R3a to R3d using climate-model output	Fit an extreme-value distribution to the Rx1day series obtained for the baseline (1986–2005) and future periods in Step R4. Given an initial design life of 10 years, the period 2016–2035 is taken as representative of future conditions. The 25-year return period estimate is derived for each ensemble member in the baseline and future periods.

continued on next page

Table 1 *continued*

Step	Activity	Viet Nam Example
R6	Derive the **change factor** for the specified design variable(s) and return period(s)	Derive the percentage change in Rx1day between the baseline and the future period—the change factor. Round up to the nearest 5% to avoid undue precision. (Note that since change in climate-model output is used, any biases are assumed to cancel each other out.)
R7	Calculate the **new design value** for the future period at the specified return period and confidence level	Multiply the observed baseline value for Rx1day (338 mm) by the change factor for the 25-year event by 2016–2035 (here rounded up to 25%) to give a design value of 423 mm at the 97.5 level of the ensemble range. The change in the upper-bound Rx1day estimate (+30%) gives 439 mm.

CMIP5 = Coupled Model Intercomparison Project, Phase 5; GEV = generalized extreme value; IPCC = Intergovernmental Panel on Climate Change; KNMI = Royal Netherlands Meteorological Institute; mm = millimeter; RCP = representative (greenhouse gas) concentration pathway.

Source: Consultant's formulation.

Mean Sea Level and High-Water Levels for Site Evaluation

The procedures for mean sea-level rise and high-water level estimation are discussed in general terms in this section. A more detailed commentary on the subject can be found in the accompanying knowledge product (ADB 2020a), together with a Further Reading list on adaptation to climate change in the coastal zone and a worked example (Appendix 3).

Sea-level component-based methods have been used elsewhere[11] and are recommended here because they are explicit about the elements included (or disregarded) in the scenario (see Further Reading section of this manual). Moreover, the sources of information can also be scrutinized more openly. Table 2 lists the most important components determining long-term local mean and extreme sea-level changes, plus short-lived high-water levels due to storms. From these, it is evident that regional and local sea-level changes may differ substantially from global mean changes. The local high-water levels given here reflect the local datum (instead of changes in high-water levels) to highlight potential risks from wave overtopping.

Table 2: Global, Regional, and Local Components of Sea-Level Change

Sea Level	Components
Global sea level	• Thermal expansion of the ocean • Greenland ice sheet surface mass balance change • Antarctic ice sheet surface mass balance change • Greenland ice sheet rapid dynamics • Antarctic ice sheet rapid dynamics • Meltwater contributions from land glaciers • Groundwater and land water storage contributions
Regional sea level	• Changes in Earth's gravity field due to redistribution of ice and water mass • Solid-Earth deformation due to redistribution of ice and water mass • Vertical land movements due to postglacial isostatic adjustment • Vertical land movements due to sedimentation, erosion, or tectonics • Subsidence due to groundwater use or compaction of sediment • Ocean circulation changes
Local high-water level	• Tidal regime • Storm surge • Maximum nearshore wave height and direction • Interacting wind, wave, tide, and surge effects • Influence of the El Niño–Southern Oscillation on water density

Source: Consultant's formulation.

---

[11] See, for example, the German Integrated Climate Data Centre: https://icdc.cen.uni-hamburg.de/1/daten/atmosphere/dwd-station.html.

For some components in Table 2, data may be difficult or even impossible to obtain. In that case, analogs, nearest locations, or published values may be used instead (e.g., Church et al. 2013; Slangen et al. 2014). Furthermore, global mean sea-level rise scenarios are revised in succeeding Intergovernmental Panel on Climate Change (IPCC) reports, so it is important to keep sources of component values under review. A fully transparent, component-based approach can make information gaps and evolving scientific understanding apparent to users of the scenarios.

Uncertainty in global sea-level change arises primarily from the future response of ice sheets to global warming, with significant transfers of mass from land to ocean and subsequent redistribution through gravitational and ocean circulation changes (Church et al. 2013). Regional sea-level change over the next few decades will be dominated by climate variability, on top of the global signal. Local changes in storm surges and waves are highly uncertain, but there is an expectation that both could increase. Sea levels are likely to rise for centuries, even millennia, to come, regardless of the outcome of mitigation policies, so an open-ended, risk-based approach to coastal planning is needed.

STEP S1: Specify project objectives.

Project objectives must be clearly stated and must specify the level of climate risk and variables involved, the economic life of the project, the amount of lock-in (irreversibility), and the degree of precaution required (ADB 2020b). In other words, it is important to begin with an understanding of the risks to project objectives, output, and outcomes, rather than with climate-model projections (which come later). Note also that the service life of large infrastructure projects may be much longer than their economic life. The time spent planning, designing, and constructing the project should also be considered.

For illustrative purposes, coastal inundation and erosion risk maps are created for the Hai Hau coast, Nam Dinh Province, on the Red River delta, northern Viet Nam. Some sections of this coast experience erosion rates in excess of 25 meters per year (Duc et al. 2017; Häglund and Svensson 2002). The variables required for coastal flood and erosion mapping are projected mean sea-level changes and high-water levels. A 10-year period for infrastructure planning, design, and construction and a service life of 90+ years are assumed, resulting in a projection horizon extending to the year 2100. Likelihood cannot be assigned to extreme (but credible) high-water levels. Sea-level changes are added to the local datum in 2000 to give absolute seawater height.

Coastline near Hon Dau on 31 July 2010

Coastline near Hon Dau on 22 December 2013

continued on next page

text box continued

Coastline near Hon Dau on 26 August 2016   Coastline near Hon Dau on 8 August 2018

The above images show coastal changes near Hon Dau on the Red River delta since 2010. Note the phase of coastal retreat between July 2010 and December 2013, followed by land reclamation completed by August 2016.

Map data: Google, CNES / Airbus, TerraMetrics.

STEP S2: Check for contextual climate risks.

Climate-risk screening should consider potential far-field as well as local threats to the proposed structure. These include the impact of climate change, both direct and indirect.

Thac Ba hydropower plant (built in 1971).   Hoa Binh hydropower plant (built in 1988).
Map data: Google, Maxar Technologies.   Map data: Google, Maxar Technologies.

In northeast Viet Nam, rivers discharge the bulk of their sediment from June to October. The dominant wind and wave direction at that time favors northward longshore currents away from Ba Lat. Historically, river sediment was deposited along the shoreline and redistributed by longshore transport. However, inland impoundments reduce the supply of river sediment to the Red River delta (Lu et al. 2015), increasing the risk of coastal erosion and inundation. For example, it is estimated that the Thac Ba reservoir (*left*) reduces the downstream sediment load by 95% (Ranzi, Le, and Rulli 2012). Local dike construction can also prevent sediment from reaching the beach. Changes in the operation of impoundments and dikes (in response to climate change) could indirectly affect the future sediment supply to the shoreline.

See the Further Reading section of this manual for an evaluation of other factors contributing to sediment budgets and erosion along the Hai Hau coast.

STEP S3: Derive a LOWER-bound mean sea level.

Following the methods adopted by the US Army Corps of Engineers,[12] the local historical rate of sea-level change is used as the lower-bound estimate. The past rate is simply extrapolated over the (economic or service) life of the infrastructure project and added to the datum. This is regarded as a lower bound because future contributions from ice melt, thermal expansion, and changes in the Earth's gravity field are expected to be greater in a warmer world than in the past. Other components such as rates of vertical land movements are assumed to remain unchanged.

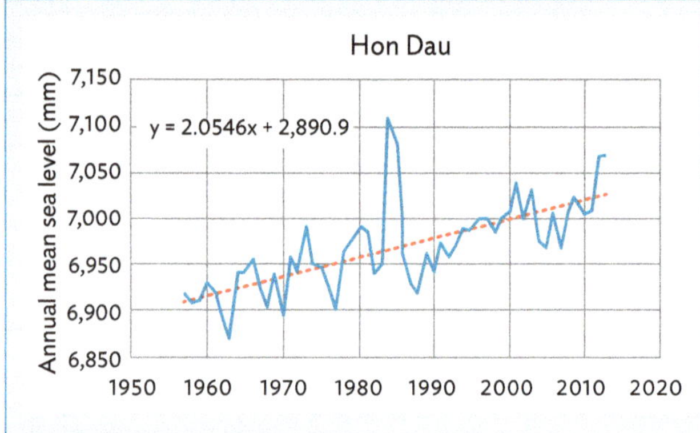

The sea-level datum for Hon Dau in the year 2000 was 7,000 mm. The observed rate of sea-level change at the site was +2.0546 mm/y over the available period of record. This yields a lower-bound sea-level estimate of 7,250 mm by 2100, after rounding up to the nearest 50 mm. Local storm surge, tide, and wave effects are not included.

Source: Consultant's formulation.

STEP S4: Derive a CENTRAL estimate of sea level including local factors.

This scenario is based on the median estimate of all sea-level change components at global, regional, and local scales (including wave, tide, and storm surge). Global components are taken from the median of the latest IPCC range (here AR5[13]), then adjusted for gravitational effects using "fingerprints" for mass transfers from the Greenland and Antarctic ice sheets to the ocean (Kopp et al. 2014). Other regional components such as postglacial isostatic adjustment, subsidence, or compaction of coastal sediment may also be included. Finally, median estimates of all locally relevant components are added to the regional change and datum to give the change in high-water level at the site.

---

[12]   http://corpsmapu.usace.army.mil/rccinfo/slc/slcc_calc.html.
[13]   Sea-level change assessed in the 5th IPCC report.

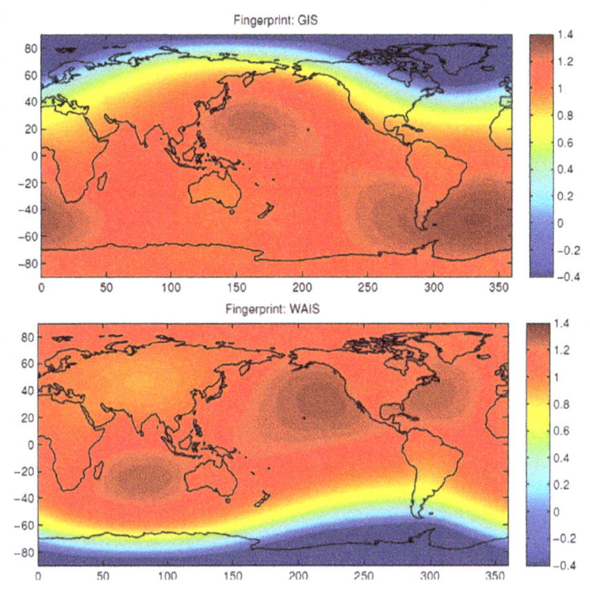

The median global sea-level change scenario based on the components in Church et al. (2013), Table 13.5, is +635 mm for RCP8.5 by 2100. Regional gravitational fingerprints of ice sheet melt in Greenland (GIS ~1.2) (upper) and the West Antarctic (WAIS ~1.05) (lower), taken from Kopp et al. (2014), add 30 mm more to the regional sea level in northern Viet Nam. Vertical land movements contribute an additional 10 mm, giving a total regional change of +675 mm.

Local tidal range increases by 20% because of the deeper water, but all other local high tide, maximum nearshore wave, and storm-surge heights are based on median estimates from observed ranges (reported for the site or the nearest location). These short-term storm surge–wave–tide elements add 9,285 mm to the regional sea-level *change* of 675 mm (on top of a datum of 7,000 mm). The result is an absolute high-water estimate of 17,000 mm, after rounding up to the nearest 50 mm.

EAIS = East Antarctic Ice Sheet, GIS = Greenland Ice Sheet, WAIS = West Antarctic Ice Sheet.
Source: Kopp, R.E., Horton, R.M., Little, C.M., Mitrovica, J.X., Oppenheimer, M., Rasmussen, D.J., Strauss, B.H. and Tebaldi, C. 2014. Probabilistic 21st and 22nd century sea-level projections at a global network of tide-gauge sites. Earth's Future, 2, 383-406.

STEP S5: Derive a HIGH estimate of sea level including local factors with component uncertainty.

This scenario begins with the same procedures as in Step 4 except that the input values for global components (adjusted for gravitational fingerprints) are taken directly from the most recent, high-end national scenario. Next, uncertainties in the components are combined using the method of quadrature (see MONRE 2016, 44). Half the combined uncertainty range is added to the median of the global components to give a high-end estimate. Likewise, uncertainties in other regional and local components are also combined by quadrature and added to their respective medians. Finally, the regional and local high-end estimates are summed, then added to the datum.

The sum of median global and regional components is +795 mm for RCP8.5 by 2100. This value is based on the values in MONRE (2016), Table 6.1, which factor in gravitational fingerprints from Slangen et al. (2014). When this change is added to half the combined uncertainty range (by quadrature), with uncertain vertical land movements, the high-end regional sea-level change becomes +1,009 mm. This value is used to adjust the local high-tide range by +202 mm (+20%, as in Step 4). Upper-bound local tide, wave, and surge heights add a further 9,150 mm, plus 1,222 mm for half their combined uncertainty range, to give a local high-water level of 11,583 mm. When the local datum is used, the absolute high-water level is 18,600 mm, after rounding up to the nearest 50 mm.

STEP S6: Derive an EXTREME estimate of sea level including local factors with component uncertainty.

Extreme, but physically plausible, upper-bound global mean sea-level change scenarios have been developed by a few agencies for use in coastal risk planning and management of long-lived critical infrastructure (e.g., Sweet et al. 2017; Environment Agency 2016; Katsman et al. 2011). These scenarios rely on a degree of expert judgment, informed by peer-reviewed scientific literature, and on credible narratives of global change. Such extreme scenarios are typically used for testing the sensitivity of engineering designs to low-probability, high-consequence events, or for identifying areas of the coastal zone that could be at risk from erosion or flooding. These are not intended to be probabilistic projections.

> Extreme global components of sea-level change and their associated uncertainty bounds are taken from Kopp et al. (2014), Table 1. This scenario assumes a large but highly uncertain contribution from melting Antarctic ice sheets. There is also a significant but uncorrelated component of ice melt from Greenland. When these and other component uncertainties are combined, the global mean sea-level change is +2,472 mm. After adjustment for gravitational fingerprints and vertical land movements, the regional sea-level change is +2,637 mm. This value is used to adjust the local tidal range by +527 mm (+20%, as in Steps 4 and 5). Historical maximum nearshore wave and surge heights added to high tide, on top of the regional sea-level change, gives a local extreme water level of 20,500 mm with respect to the datum (after rounding up to the nearest 50 mm).

As with the change factors for extreme rainfall, simplifying assumptions are also made when calculating sea-level change. The most important caveats are as follows: (i) extreme surge and wave heights will remain the same; (ii) extreme surges, waves, and tides will behave independently of one another; (iii) vertical land movements due to tectonic processes, groundwater exploitation, or changes in coastal sediment budgets can be disregarded (except for the lower-bound example); and (iv) coastal morphology and bathymetry will be unchanged. All this means that the extreme sea-level change estimate could be even higher than what is shown here.

Table 3: Steps in Estimating Mean Sea Level and High-Water Levels at a Site

Step	Activity	Viet Nam Example
S1	Specify project **objectives**	Assess risk of coastal flooding and erosion up to 2100 to support land-use planning and asset management along a rapidly eroding section of the north Viet Nam coast.
S2	Check for **contextual climate risks**	Recognize that local rates of erosion are determined partly by sediment supplied by regulated rivers, and that climate change may disrupt the operation of impoundments or alter downstream sediment sources or transport mechanisms.
S3	Derive a **LOWER-bound** mean sea-level change estimate from the trend in historical tide records	For the nearest available tide gauge: (a) Obtain the historical annual mean sea-level series, checking to make sure that it has been adjusted to a revised local reference level by the Permanent Service for Mean Sea Level; (b) Fit a linear regression line to the historical series and obtain the gradient term (mm/year); (c) Extrapolate the gradient to the end of the analysis period (here 2100); (d) Add the expected change in sea level to the local datum (7,000 mm); and (e) Round up, using the tolerance value (here 50 mm). Here the expected LOWER-bound mean sea level (excluding tide, wave, and storm effects) is 7,250 mm by 2100.

continued on next page

Table 3 *continued*

Step	Activity	Viet Nam Example
S4	Derive a **CENTRAL estimate** of sea level including local factors but excluding component uncertainty	Refer to the most recent table of global mean sea-level change components issued by the IPCC for the chosen RCP: (a) Calculate the sum of the median values for global sea-level change components (e.g., thermal expansion); (b) Apply gravitational fingerprints to the Antarctic and Greenland ice melt contributions to obtain regional levels; (c) Add the median estimates of other regional components (e.g., vertical land movements); (d) Adjust the local tidal range using a factor applied to (c); (e) Add the median estimates of local components (e.g., high tide, nearshore wave, and surge heights); (f) Add (e) to the datum to obtain the local water level; and (g) Round up, using the tolerance value (here 50 mm). Here the expected CENTRAL sea level (including tide, wave, and storm effects) is 17,000 mm by 2100.
S5	Derive a **HIGH estimate** of sea level including local factors with component uncertainty	Refer to the most recent table of global mean sea-level change components and uncertainties issued by the IPCC (or national agencies) for the chosen RCP: (a) Follow the same procedure as in S4 but at steps (a), (c), and (e) add half the combined component uncertainty estimated by quadrature for global, regional, and local components, respectively; (b) Add the sum of regional and local components in (a) to the datum; and (c) Round up, using the tolerance value (here 50 mm). Here the expected HIGH sea level (including tide, wave, and storm effects with component uncertainty at all scales) is 18,600 mm by 2100.
S6	Derive an **EXTREME estimate** of sea level including local factors with component uncertainty	Refer to credible sources of extreme global mean sea-level components and accompanying narratives for the chosen RCP: (a) Follow the same procedure as in S5 but use the most extreme values for all components with attendant uncertainty ranges; (b) Add the sum of regional and local components in (a) to the datum; and (c) Round up, using the tolerance value (here 50 mm). Here the expected EXTREME sea level (including tide, wave, and storm effects with component uncertainty at all scales) is 20,500 mm by 2100.

IPCC = Intergovernmental Panel on Climate Change, mm = millimeter, RCP = representative (greenhouse gas) concentration pathway.

Source: Consultant's formulation.

4 Concluding Remarks

This manual describes step-by-step procedures for applying climate change adjustments to extreme-rainfall and local sea-level estimates. The overall approach (with accompanying worked examples and spreadsheets) is intended to be as transparent as possible. All sources of information and assumptions should be open to scrutiny, given the large uncertainty and rapidly advancing science behind some elements. Input values should be periodically reviewed and refreshed, at least in line with the latest IPCC reports and national scenarios.

Some data may be impossible to obtain for project site(s), so it is often necessary to refer to nearest-neighbor records or to published values. Again, transparent procedures will reveal where such knowledge gaps exist and highlight opportunities for further research. Unfortunately, there is as yet no single source or platform for obtaining all the climate change information needed for detailed engineering design. Fragmentary evidence can also lead to a lack of internal consistency among the data, which, in turn, will hinder efforts to attach return periods to some derived quantities.

Finally, there is a limit to what can be achieved through generic guidance when allowing for site-specific climate threats in DED. Nonetheless, the underlying principles and procedures set out in this manual offer points of departure for more sophisticated assessments of high-risk projects.

References

Allen, M. R., and W. J. Ingram. 2002. Constraints on Future Changes in Climate and the Hydrologic Cycle. *Nature*. 419. pp. 228–232.

Asian Development Bank (ADB). 2018. *Project Preparatory Technical Assistance Report: Adjusting Hydrological Inputs to Road Design for Climate Change Risk Based on Extreme Value Analysis*. Manila (PPTA 8957-VIE).

———. 2020a. *Climate-Change Adjustments for Detailed Engineering Design: With Worked Examples from Viet Nam*. Manila.

———. 2020b. *Principles for Updating the ADB Climate Risk Management (CRM) and Climate Risk and Adaptation Assessments (CRAs)*. Manila.

Australian Bureau of Meteorology (ABOM) and Commonwealth Scientific and Industrial Research Organisation (CSIRO). 2014. *Climate Variability, Extremes and Change in the Western Tropical Pacific: New Science and Updated Country Reports*. Pacific-Australia Climate Change Science and Adaptation Planning Program Technical Report. Melbourne: ABOM and CSIRO.

Chen, C., M. A. Cane, A. T. Wittenberg, and D. Chen. 2017. ENSO in the CMIP5 Simulations: Life Cycles, Diversity, and Responses to Climate Change. *Journal of Climate*. 30 (2). pp. 775–801.

Church, J. A., P. U. Clark, A. Cazenave, J. M. Gregory, S. Jevrejeva, A. Levermann, M. A. Merrifield, G. A. Milne, R. S. Nerem, P. D. Nunn, A. J. Payne, W. T. Pfeffer, D. Stammer, and A.S. Unnikrishnan. 2013. Sea Level Change. In: Stocker, T. F., D. Qin, G.-K. Plattner, M. Tignor, S. K. Allen, J. Boschung, A. Nauels, Y. Xia, V. Bex, and P. M. Midgley, eds. *Climate Change 2013: The Physical Science Basis; Contribution of Working Group I to the Fifth Assessment Report of the Intergovernmental Panel on Climate Change*. Cambridge University Press.

Dasgupta, S., B. Laplante, C. Meisner, D. Wheeler, and J. Yan. 2009a. The Impact of Sea Level Rise on Developing Countries: A Comparative Analysis. *Climatic Change*. 93 (3–4). pp. 379–388.

Dasgupta, S., B. Laplante, S. Murray, and D. Wheeler. 2009b. Sea-Level Rise and Storm Surges: A Comparative Analysis of Impacts in Developing Countries. *Policy Research Working Paper*. No. WPS 4901. Washington, DC: World Bank.

Deser, C., A. S. Phillips, M. A. Alexander, and B. V. Smoliak. 2014. Projecting North American Climate over the Next 50 Years: Uncertainty due to Internal Variability. *Journal of Climate*. 27 (6). pp. 2,271–2,296.

Duc, D. M., K. Yasuhara, N. M. Hieu, and N. C. Lan. 2017. Climate Change Impacts on a Large-Scale Erosion Coast of Hai Hau District, Vietnam and the Adaptation. *Journal of Coastal Conservation.* 21 (1). pp. 47–62.

Environment Agency, UK. 2016. *Adapting to Climate Change: Advice for Flood and Coastal Erosion Risk Management Authorities.* Bristol, England.

Flato, G., J. Marotzke, B. Abiodun, P. Braconnot, S. C. Chou, W. Collins, P. Cox, F. Driouech, S. Emori, V. Eyring, C. Forest, P. Gleckler, E. Guilyardi, C. Jakob, V. Kattsov, C. Reason, and M. Rummukainen. 2013. Evaluation of Climate Models. In: Stocker, T. F., D. Qin, G.-K. Plattner, M. Tignor, S. K. Allen, J. Boschung, A. Nauels, Y. Xia, V. Bex, and P. M. Midgley, eds. *Climate Change 2013: The Physical Science Basis; Contribution of Working Group I to the Fifth Assessment Report of the Intergovernmental Panel on Climate Change.* Cambridge University Press.

Guerreiro, S. B., H. J. Fowler, R. Barbero, S. Westra, G. Lenderink, S. Blenkinsop, E. Lewis, and X-F. Li. 2018. Detection of Continental-Scale Intensification of Hourly Rainfall Extremes. *Nature Climate Change.* 8 (9). pp. 803–807.

Häglund, M., and P. Svensson. 2002. *Coastal Erosion at Hai Hau Beach in the Red River Delta, Vietnam.* Master of Science thesis in Coastal Engineering. Division of Water Resources Engineering, Lund University, Sweden.

Hawkins, E., and R. Sutton. 2010. The Potential to Narrow Uncertainty in Projections of Regional Precipitation Change. *Climate Dynamics.* 37 (1–2). pp. 407–418.

Katsman, C. A., A. Sterl, J. J. Beersma, H. W. van den Brink, J. A. Church, W. Hazeleger, R. E. Kopp, D. Kroon, J. Kwadijk, R. Lammersen, J. Lowe, M. Oppenheimer, H.-P. Plag, J. Ridley, H. von Storch, D. G. Vaughan, P. Vellinga, L. L. A. Vermeersen, R. S. W. van de Wal, and R. Weisse. 2011. Exploring High-End Scenarios for Local Sea Level Rise to Develop Flood Protection Strategies for a Low-Lying Delta—The Netherlands as an Example. *Climatic Change.* 109 (3–4). pp. 617–645.

Katzfey, J. J., J. L. McGregor, and R. Suppiah. 2014. *High-Resolution Climate Projections for Vietnam: Technical Report.* Commonwealth Scientific and Industrial Research Organisation (CSIRO), Australia.

Knutti, R., R. Furrer, C. Tebaldi, J. Cermak, and G. A. Meehl. 2010. Challenges in Combining Projections from Multiple Climate Models. *Journal of Climate.* 23 (10). pp. 2739–2758.

Kopp, R. E., R. M. Horton, C. M. Little, J. X. Mitrovica, M. Oppenheimer, D. J. Rasmussen, B. H. Strauss, and C. Tebaldi. 2014. Probabilistic 21st and 22nd Century Sea-Level Projections at a Global Network of Tide-Gauge Sites. *Earth's Future.* 2 (8). pp. 383–406.

Lu, X. X., C. Oeurng, T. P. Q. Le, and D. T. Thuy. 2015. Sediment Budget as Affected by Construction of a Sequence of Dams in the Lower Red River, Viet Nam. *Geomorphology.* 248. pp. 125–133.

McSweeney, C. F., R. G. Jones, R. W. Lee, and D. P. Rowell. 2015. Selecting CMIP5 GCMs for Downscaling over Multiple Regions. *Climate Dynamics.* 44 (11–12). pp. 3,237–3,260.

Ministry of Natural Resources and Environment (MONRE), Viet Nam. 2016. *Climate Change and Sea Level Rise Scenarios for Viet Nam.* Prepared by the Viet Nam Institute of Meteorology, Hydrology and Climate Change, Ha Noi.

Pielke, R. A., Sr., and R. L. Wilby. 2012. Regional Climate Downscaling: What's the Point? *Eos.* 93 (5). pp. 52–53.

Racherla, P. N., D. T. Shindell, and G. S. Faluvegi. 2012. The Added Value to Global Model Projections of Climate Change by Dynamical Downscaling: A Case Study over the Continental U.S. Using the GISS-ModelIE2 and WRF Models. *Journal of Geophysical Research: Atmospheres.* 117. D20118.

Ranzi, R., T. H. Le, and M. C. Rulli. 2012. A RUSLE Approach to Model Suspended Sediment Load in the Lo River (Vietnam): Effects of Reservoirs and Land Use Changes. *Journal of Hydrology.* 422–423. pp. 17–29.

Slangen, A. B. A., M. Carson, C. A. Katsman, R. S. W. Van de Wal, A. Köhl, L. L. A. Vermeersen, and D. Stammer. 2014. Projecting Twenty-First Century Regional Sea-Level Changes. *Climatic Change.* 124 (1–2). pp. 317–332.

Sweet, W. V., R. E. Kopp, C. P. Weaver, J. Obeysekera, R. M. Horton, E. R. Thieler, and C. Zervas. 2017. *Global and Regional Sea Level Rise Scenarios for the United States.* National Oceanic and Atmospheric Administration (NOAA) Technical Report NOS CO-OPS 083. Maryland: NOAA/NOS Center for Operational Oceanographic Products and Services.

Taylor, K. E., R. J. Stouffer, and G. A. Meehl. 2012. An Overview of CMIP5 and the Experiment Design. *Bulletin of the American Meteorological Society.* 93 (4). pp. 485–498.

Yun, K. S., S. W. Yeh, and K. J. Ha. 2016. Inter-El Niño Variability in CMIP5 Models: Model Deficiencies and Future Changes. *Journal of Geophysical Research: Atmospheres.* 121 (8). pp. 3,894–3,906.

Further Reading

Asian Development Bank (ADB). 2018. Information Sources to Support ADB Climate Risk Assessment and Management. Technical Note. Manila: Asian Development Bank. https://www.adb.org/publications/adb-climate-risk-assessments-information-sources. **A compendium of open-access sources of data including historical weather information and climate-model output.**

Hoan, L. X., H. Hanson, M. Larson, C. Donnelly, and P. T. Nam. 2010. Modeling Shoreline Evolution at Hai Hau Beach, Vietnam. *Journal of Coastal Research*. 26 (1). pp. 31–43. **A demonstration of modeling techniques for evaluating hypotheses of the causes of rapid coastal erosion in Hai Hau District, Viet Nam.**

Menabde, M., A. Seed, and G. Pegram. 1999. A Simple Scaling Model for Extreme Rainfall. *Water Resources Research*. 35 (1). pp. 335–339. **A seminal paper showing how extreme sub-daily rainfall intensities can be scaled from daily totals.**

Nicholls, R. J., S. E. Hanson, J. A. Lowe, R. A. Warrick, X. Lu, and A. J. Long. 2014. Sea-Level Scenarios for Evaluating Coastal Impacts. *Wiley Interdisciplinary Reviews (WIREs) Climate Change*. 5 (1). pp. 129–150. **A review of the various mechanisms contributing to local sea-level change, with a proposed pragmatic methodology for combining available data to create local (relative) sea-level rise scenarios.**

Su, H. T., and Y. K. Tung. 2013. Incorporating Uncertainty of Distribution Parameters due to Sampling Errors in Flood-Damage-Reduction Project Evaluation. *Water Resources Research*. 49 (3). pp. 1680–1692. **A presentation of straightforward procedures for calculating the standard error of a Gumbel extreme-value estimate, given only the scale parameter and the required return period.**

Westra, S., H. J. Fowler, J. P. Evans, L. V. Alexander, P. Berg, F. Johnson, E. J. Kendon, G. Lenderink, and N. M. Roberts. 2014. Future Changes to the Intensity and Frequency of Short-Duration Extreme Rainfall. *Reviews of Geophysics*. 52 (3). pp. 522–555. **A review of the evidence and physical basis of sub-daily extreme-rainfall intensification due to anthropogenic climate change.**

Wilby, R. L., N. J. Clifford, P. De Luca, S. O. Harrigan, J. K. Hillier, R. Hodgkins, M. F. Johnson, T. K. R. Matthews, C. Murphy, S. J. Noone, S. Parry, C. Prudhomme, S. P. Rice, L. J. Slater, K. A. Smith, and P. J. Wood. 2017. The "Dirty Dozen" of Freshwater Science: Detecting Then Reconciling Hydrological Data Biases and Errors. *Wiley Interdisciplinary Reviews (WIREs) Water*. 4 (3). https://doi.org/10.1002/wat2.1209. **A description of typical signs of suspect hydro-meteorological data, along with examples of common data handling and archiving issues.**